The 30-Day Inspirational Journal
for young entrepreneurs

Believe in Yourself!
Get excited! your best days
are ahead!
–Solomon

Printed in the United States of America

First Printing, June 2016

ISBN: 978-1533685209

Habakkuk Publishing
Canton, Michigan

Dedication

This book is dedicated to my mother and father, Andrea and Michael Dudley. Your unwavering belief in me is helping me to soar. I love you both.

From the Author

How to use the
30 Day Inspirational Journal for Young Entrepreneurs

Thank you for purchasing the 30 Day Inspirational journal for Young Entrepreneurs. It is created as a place for young entrepreneurs to write your thoughts, experiences and observations. It is designed for you to write daily. Use whatever writing tool you desire, whether it is a pen or a pencil. It's entirely up to you.

Journaling is all about you and your thoughts. Journaling is very private...so feel free to write your deepest most intimate thoughts.

Each page in the journal is broken down into three divisions:

1) Today I was inspired by, 2) I am most grateful for and
3) Tomorrow I'm looking forward to. Take 10 minutes out every day to reflect on how and what inspired you. Treasure every day. Life moves by very quickly and while it seems like it may be moving slowly now, I guarantee you...it moves fast.

Expressing gratitude for your blessings is one of the keys to happiness and success in life. Brian Tracy says this about gratitude, "Develop an attitude of gratitude, and give thanks for everything that happens to you, knowing that every step forward is a step toward achieving something bigger and better than your current situation."

Finally, forecasting the future by writing what you want and expect your life to look like is essential to living a great life, filled with fulfilled dreams and goals. Proverbs 29:18 says, "If people can't see what God is doing, they stumble all over themselves; But when they attend to what he reveals, they are most blessed", The Message Bible.

Journaling can change your life. It keeps you accountable and can help to direct your thoughts. I suggest spending 10 minutes a day journaling. As a young entrepreneur those 10 minutes...away from your electronic devices and social media, can connect you with you again.

Happy Journaling,

Solomon X. Dudley
#YoungWiseMan

day 1

Today I was inspired by...

_____

_____

_____

I am most grateful for...

_____

_____

_____

Tomorrow I'm looking forward to...

_____

_____

_____

I say I am stronger than fear.
- Malala Yousafzai

day 2

Today I was inspired by...

_____

_____

_____

I am most grateful for...

_____

_____

_____

Tomorrow I'm looking forward to...

_____

_____

_____

"If you are born poor its not your fault,
But if you die poor its your mistake."
- Bill Gates

day 3

Today I was inspired by...

_____

_____

_____

I am most grateful for...

_____

_____

_____

Tomorrow I'm looking forward to...

_____

_____

_____

"You are the designer of your destiny;
you are the author of your story."
- Lisa Nichols

day 4

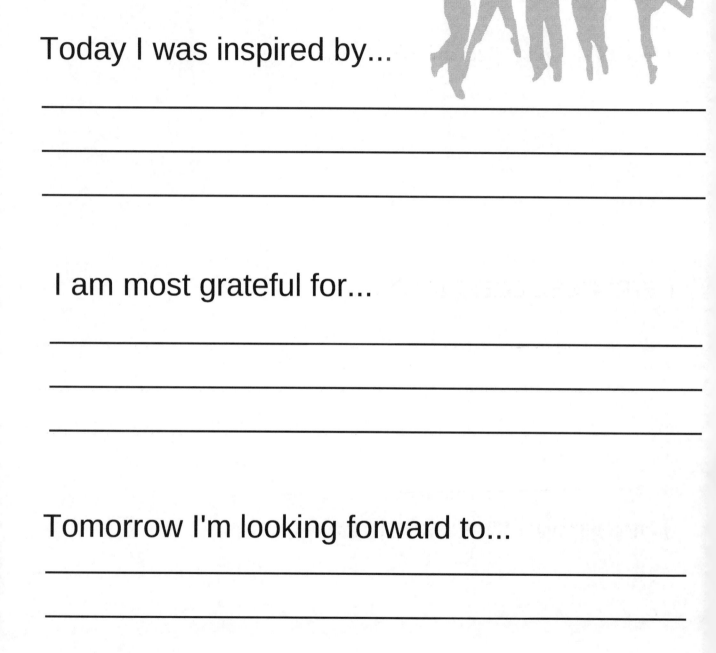

Today I was inspired by...

_____

_____

_____

I am most grateful for...

_____

_____

_____

Tomorrow I'm looking forward to...

_____

_____

_____

"Stay loyal to your creativity."
- Pharell

day 5

Today I was inspired by...

_____

_____

_____

I am most grateful for...

_____

_____

_____

Tomorrow I'm looking forward to...

_____

_____

_____

"I dare you to be great! I challenge you to be
great in every single thing you do!"
- Eric Thomas

day 6

Today I was inspired by...

_____

_____

_____

I am most grateful for...

_____

_____

_____

Tomorrow I'm looking forward to...

_____

_____

_____

"Believe you can and you're
halfway there."
- Theodore Roosevelt

day 7

Today I was inspired by...

_____

_____

_____

I am most grateful for...

_____

_____

_____

Tomorrow I'm looking forward to...

_____

_____

_____

"Be humble. Be hungry. Always be the
hardest worker in the room."
- Dwayne "the Rock" Johnson

day 8

Today I was inspired by...

_____

_____

_____

I am most grateful for...

_____

_____

_____

Tomorrow I'm looking forward to...

_____

_____

_____

"I knew I had to make a sacrifice to
do what I've always wanted to do."
- Brandy Norwood

day 9

Today I was inspired by...

_____

_____

_____

I am most grateful for...

_____

_____

_____

Tomorrow I'm looking forward to...

_____

_____

_____

"Build your dreams, or someone
else will hire you to build theirs."
- Eric Thomas

day 10

Today I was inspired by...

_____

_____

_____

I am most grateful for...

_____

_____

_____

Tomorrow I'm looking forward to...

_____

_____

_____

"Faith is taking the first step even if you
do not see the whole staircase."
- Dr. Martin Luther King, Jr.

day 11

Today I was inspired by...

_____

_____

_____

I am most grateful for...

_____

_____

_____

Tomorrow I'm looking forward to...

_____

_____

_____

"See yourself living in abundance and you will attract it.
It always works, it works every time with every person."
- Bob Proctor

day 12

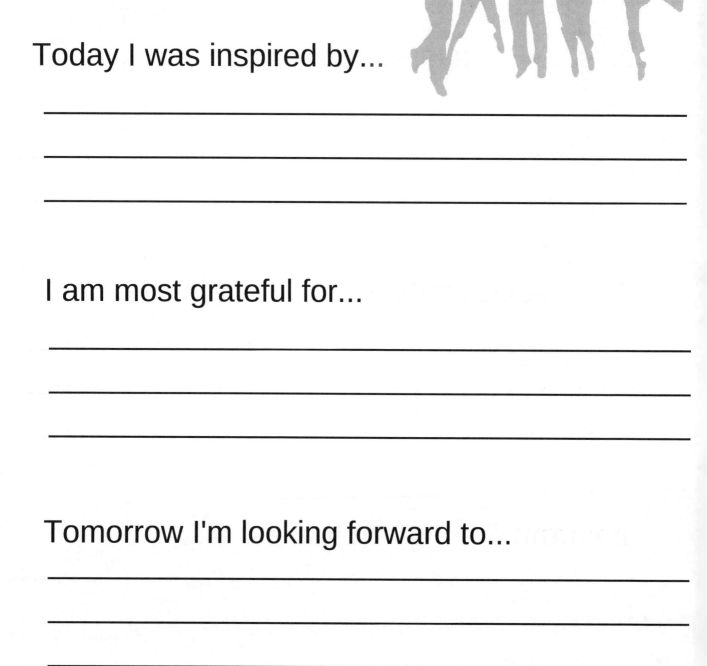

Today I was inspired by...

_____

_____

_____

I am most grateful for...

_____

_____

_____

Tomorrow I'm looking forward to...

_____

_____

_____

"Your posture in this season will
determine your placement in the next."
- Tye Tribbett

day 13

Today I was inspired by...

_____

_____

_____

I am most grateful for...

_____

_____

_____

Tomorrow I'm looking forward to...

_____

_____

_____

"But out of limitations comes creativity."
- Debbie Allen

day 14

Today I was inspired by...

_____

_____

_____

I am most grateful for...

_____

_____

_____

Tomorrow I'm looking forward to...

_____

_____

_____

"Wheresoever you go, go with all
your heart."
- Confucius

day 15

Today I was inspired by...

_____

_____

_____

I am most grateful for...

_____

_____

_____

Tomorrow I'm looking forward to...

_____

_____

_____

"It takes courage to grow up and
become who you really are."
- E.E. Cummings

day 16

Today I was inspired by...

_____

_____

_____

I am most grateful for...

_____

_____

_____

Tomorrow I'm looking forward to...

_____

_____

_____

"Life is a blank canvas You are the painter
and hence the paintbrush is your hand."
- Pharrell

day 17

Today I was inspired by...

_____

_____

_____

I am most grateful for...

_____

_____

_____

Tomorrow I'm looking forward to...

_____

_____

_____

"If you take responsibility for yourself you will
develop a hunger to accomplish your dreams."
- Les Brown

day 18

Today I was inspired by...

_____

_____

_____

I am most grateful for...

_____

_____

_____

Tomorrow I'm looking forward to...

_____

_____

_____

"Average minds analyze. Great minds execute."
- Lewis Howes

day 19

Today I was inspired by...

_____

_____

_____

I am most grateful for...

_____

_____

_____

Tomorrow I'm looking forward to...

_____

_____

_____

"You can dream big and it doesn't matter
what you look like, where you come from."
- Misty Copeland

day 20

Today I was inspired by...

_____

_____

_____

I am most grateful for...

_____

_____

_____

Tomorrow I'm looking forward to...

_____

_____

_____

"It's kind of fun to do the impossible."
- Walt Disney

day 21

Today I was inspired by...

_____

_____

_____

I am most grateful for...

_____

_____

_____

Tomorrow I'm looking forward to...

_____

_____

_____

"Whether you think you can, or think you
can't, you're probably right."
– Henry Ford

day 22

Today I was inspired by...

_____

_____

_____

I am most grateful for...

_____

_____

_____

Tomorrow I'm looking forward to...

_____

_____

_____

"You must be the change you
wish to see in the world."
- Gandhi

day 23

Today I was inspired by...

_____

_____

_____

I am most grateful for...

_____

_____

_____

Tomorrow I'm looking forward to...

_____

_____

_____

"Always be courageous and don't fear."
- Gabby Douglas

day 24

Today I was inspired by...

_____

_____

_____

I am most grateful for...

_____

_____

_____

Tomorrow I'm looking forward to...

_____

_____

_____

"I am overly ambitious because I
realize it can be done."
- Pharrell

day 25

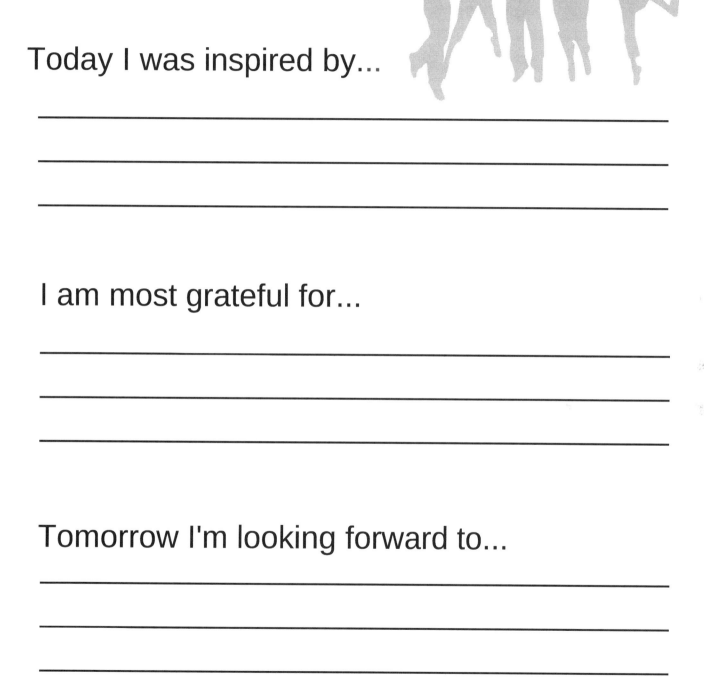

Today I was inspired by...

_____

_____

_____

I am most grateful for...

_____

_____

_____

Tomorrow I'm looking forward to...

_____

_____

_____

"No matter where you're from,
your dreams are valid."
- Lupita Nyong'o

day 26

Today I was inspired by...

_____

_____

_____

I am most grateful for...

_____

_____

_____

Tomorrow I'm looking forward to...

_____

_____

_____

"Keep your head up, your spirit strong, and continue
to develop an achievement driven mindset."
- Les Brown

day 27

Today I was inspired by...

_____

_____

_____

I am most grateful for...

_____

_____

_____

Tomorrow I'm looking forward to...

_____

_____

_____

"Apply the ABC's of success to your
life. Ask, Believe, and Claim It!"
- Eric Thomas

day 28

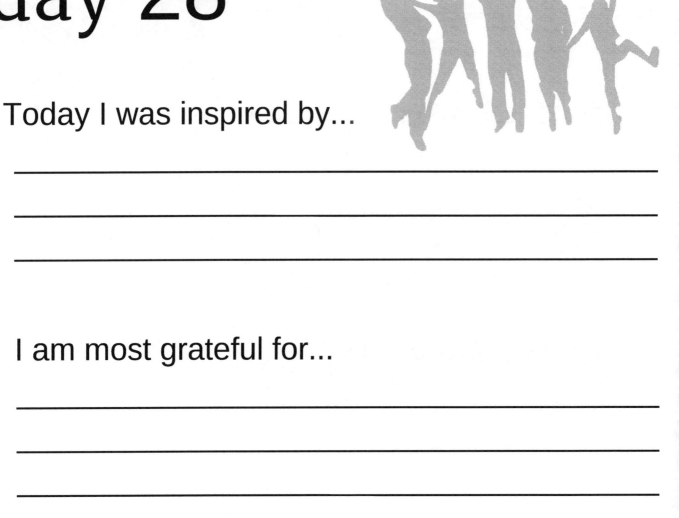

Today I was inspired by...

_____

_____

_____

I am most grateful for...

_____

_____

_____

Tomorrow I'm looking forward to...

_____

_____

_____

"Embrace your extraordinary!"
- Unknown

day 29

Today I was inspired by...

_____

_____

_____

I am most grateful for...

_____

_____

_____

Tomorrow I'm looking forward to...

_____

_____

_____

"I'm one of those people that doesn't
"follow trends". I set them."
- Zendaya

day 30

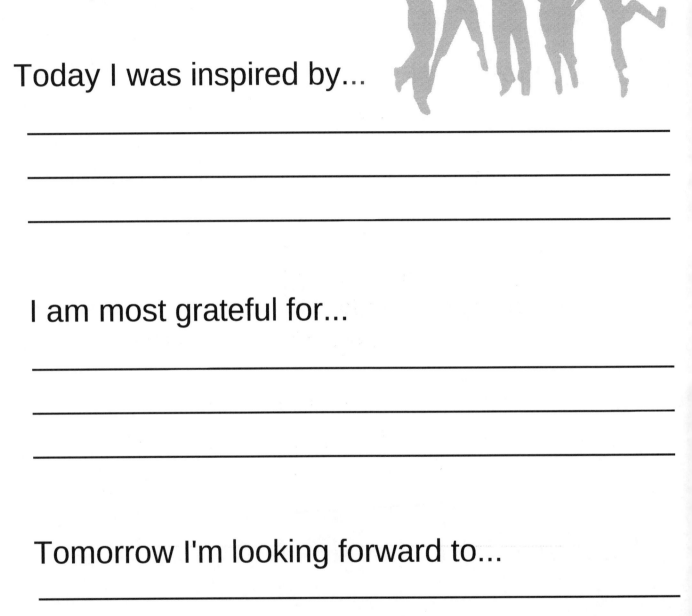

Today I was inspired by...

_____

_____

_____

I am most grateful for...

_____

_____

_____

Tomorrow I'm looking forward to...

_____

_____

_____

Don't stop dreaming, loving and creating, but most of all,
believing in yourself. Your big moment is right around the corner!
Solomon Dudley

About the Author

Solomon Dudley, also known as #YoungWiseMan, is a goal-driven individual. A graduate of Canton High School, his aspirations are to continue inspiring others through social media, on stage, and through one-on-one interaction.

His mentors include: Sandi Krakowski, Marshawn Evans, Les Brown, and Bob Proctor. Solomon has many goals, dreams, and aspirations. He sees himself inspiring millions of teens and young adults to become the best person that they can be.

In the near future, Solomon will attend college where he will continue to live life to the fullest on a daily basis. He loves traveling and has visited Greece, Israel and Africa.

Acknowledgements

Before you leave, I would like to thank you, the young entrepreneur, for taking time to write your thoughts down. I hope the past thirty days have been transformational, uplifting, and epic! Thank you for wanting to become a better individual. Your efforts will not go unnoticed!

Secondly, I would like to thank my parents who have made writing this journal an easy process. First, I thank God for my mom. She is my business partner and biggest supporter! I have always gotten fresh ideas and ways to inspire audiences. Without her, I am uncertain of where I would be. I would also like to thank my dad for also encouraging and inspiring me to stay strong and positive throughout the process of preparing this journal for you. Together, my parents have been my biggest supporters and cheerleaders.

Thank you,
Solomon X. Dudley, #YoungWiseMan

Made in the USA
San Bernardino, CA
30 June 2016